Lift High the Candle

Heather Strickler

Wyrd Bard Tales

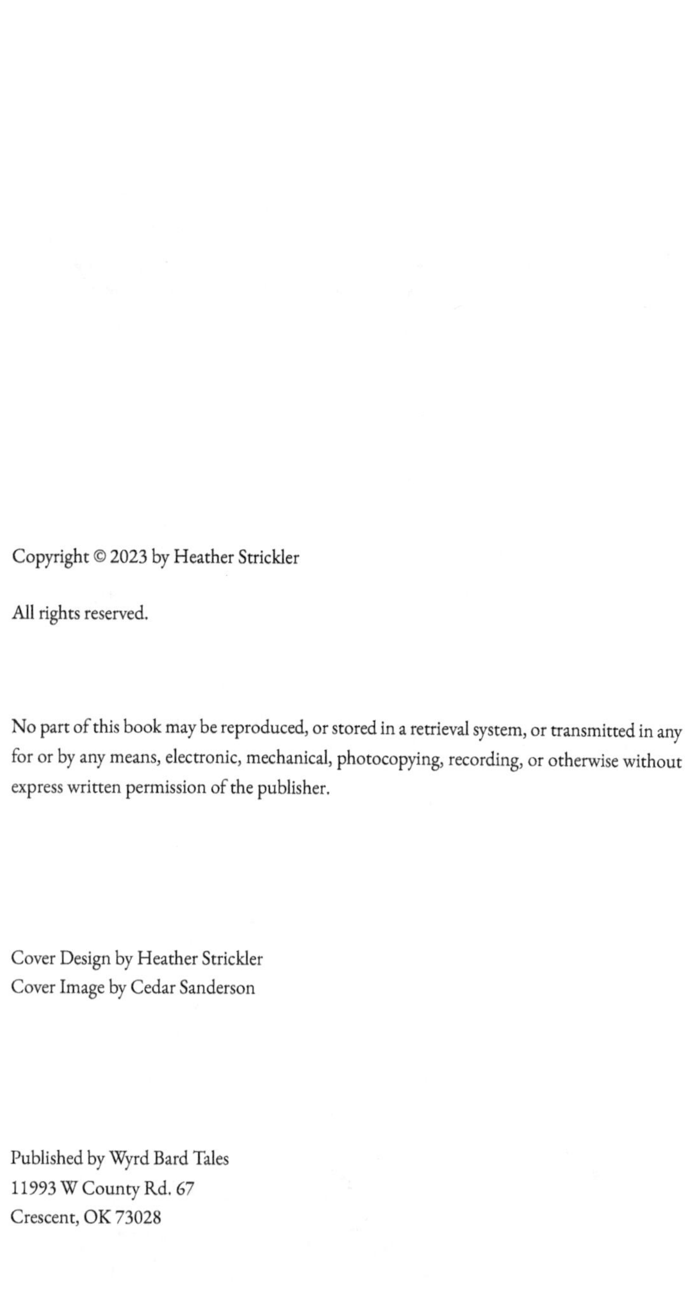

Cover Design by Heather Strickler
Cover Image by Cedar Sanderson

Published by Wyrd Bard Tales
11993 W County Rd. 67
Crescent, OK 73028

Contents

Preface

This was a book that wasn't really supposed to be. While I have always doodled around with poetry, I had not considered putting together a book like this. I had occasionally posted a poem here or there, ("Look up" was one of these from 2016).

Then in 2020, an online acquaintance (I wish I knew her well enough to call her friend, alas) lost a beloved pet with a storied life. And a poem struck me as they some times do. I posted the 'For Greebo' Poem for her, and was surprised by the positive reception not just from her.

I thought that would be the end of it, but it wasn't. Starting in the end of 2021 more of them started coming out, posted on the same blog. Mostly by fits and starts, but with increasing frequency.

Somewhere around the 2022 elections several people on that blog asked me to collect the poems and asked where they could buy them. So... this book came to be. Many of them started life on the blog mentioned above (AccordingtoHoyt for the curious) some have been posted on my own, and a few are entirely new, but this is the first time they are all together.

I hope it brings you a tiny touch of hope and light to your heart no matter how dark the days.

~Heather Strickler

For Greebo

A shadow passes by Valhalla;
   The grim doors clear the way.
The tales, the tuna, they call him,
But he scorns the lost battle's day.

The skalds chant out his deeds,
But blithely he passes them by.
There are other voices he heeds,
Voices that to a weary warrior cry.

He finds next a gate of gold,
Beside it a book and chair.
A kindly man beckons him,
And the shadow comes to stare.

"Come here, come here, sir shadow,
Ye echo of a soul,
You gave of yourself so greatly,
Come, rest, and be made whole.

"Your Lady will yet come for you.

Come rest and bide the days.
We have sent others to stand sentry,
And guard her in her ways."

The shadow nodded slowly
And joined the family line,
Of those shadows who awaited
The sharing of life divine.

And Peter turned from the throng of shadows,
To the long and biding queue,
And one by one souls entered,
And the shadows who still knew them, turned souls and entered, too.

The Leaving

W hy must I leave the home of my heart?
Why can't I stay? Why must we part?
The sun set is passing... why must it be mine?

To friends in the mourning I drink a last toast.
To friends in the evening, I play a last host.
The sunset is passing, it almost is time.

Each memory I carry, a slow trail of days.
Each thing I bear with me, an echo of ways.
The sun set is passing. What stands in my way?

To a new home I wander, reluctant feet slow.
To a new home I wander, new friends to known.
The sun set is passing. Still comes the new day.

Memories of Grief

A memory in a cup.
Drink it down, hold it up.

That day, a day in history.
What it means, we've yet to see.

Lift your eyes to the sky,
Lift your prayers and hold them high.

Distill the truth to memory
Pour the wine, let it flow free.

Joy of Memory

I drink to the past that lives only in dreams,

And a world that is never quite what it seems.

Beggars on high prance worse than kings,

But the future is spun from fanciful things.

Raise a glass to the past,

Raise a glass to the sky.

Such times never last.

Raise your glasses up high.

Glory has faded, and hope seems so dim,

Yet, laughter still rises even when things are grim.

A spark here of hope, a glimmer of faith,

And a moment of glory shines on our face.

Raise a glass to the past,

Raise a glass to the sky.

Such times never last.

Raise your glasses up high.

The darkness grows blacker. The storm looms above.

The joy of the making, shelters the love.
The love of the craft, and the joy of the soul,
Reach out to that past, and make that time whole.

Raise a glass to the past,
Raise a glass to the sky.
The joy still will last,
Raise your glasses up high.

Summer's End

The golden summer glow
Fades to autumn's golden leaves.
Then the first hints of snow
Shine silver on the eaves.

The future lies in shadow,
But the fire now is warm.
The harvest is uncertain,
But my heart still is calm.

When comes the storm before us?
When blows the bitter wind?
It comes like each day dawning
And goes with each night's end.

Look up, hope shines above you,
It never fades away.
The storm can only hide it,
Never blow its light away.

Light a Simple Candle

Light a simple candle,
    For days again are dark.
Light a simple candle,
As wolves and jackals bark.

Light a simple candle
Then lift up your soul
In prayer both bold and humble
To make our nation whole.

Light a simple candle
Lift your voice to sing.
Bring hope unto the weary
Unto the broken sing.

Light a simple candle
Enough to show the way.
Enough to ease the darkness
Until the break of day.

Dark Days

In a bleak and barren landscape,
A candle raises high.
In the stillness of the sorrow,
It still has yet to die.

We are not yet abandoned,
Though the bitter scene is cold
The light is not extinguished
From the candles that we hold.

The angry voices raging
For a moment they are still,
And all creation stops and listens
To a single will.

What is now unfolding
No prophets are here to see.
Yet the candle is uplifted
For wounded liberty.

Dark days now lay before us.

Dark souls have gathered 'round.
But the candles are still burning.
And a pathway will be found.

What awaits us on the pathway,
Still no safe can know,
There is no other option,
We must arise and go.

The option is not waiting,
But laying down to die.
We must yet keep on moving
With our candles lifted high.

Edge of the Storm

The storm clouds billow overhead
    The flood laps at my feet.
The lightnings flash with looming dread,
As I the tempest meet.

Yet I stand here, not alone,
But with blooming host beside.
The hidden war all but done,
Just left where the shadows hide.

There is a stillness in my breast
That I cannot explain,
Save that the ever-present rest
Has joined me yet again.

In shadows move, not just the foe,
But ten thousand friends besides,
We cannot count their number so,
But in their hands the tide.

I raise my head to to storm clouds black,

And stark against the gloom,
A single ray of lights fights back,
And spells the darkness' doom.

Powers move in the unseen places,
And those powers that I see,
Have shining swords and radiant faces,
Turned against our enemy.

Lift High the Candle

What do you do when the world all comes down?
When the path of devastation is all that can be found?
What do you do when it all turns black and cold?
And the only light around you is the candle that you hold?

Lift high the candle, first above all else.
Lift high the candle, even if this fails.
Lift high the candle, strong against the dark.
Lift high the candle, look for glimmers, small and stark.

There are other candles, and together they still come.
Here and there one flickers, then falls to darkness's hum,
But still they come together, a silent chorus of strength
And so assay the damage, the storm left in its wake.

Lift high the candle, first the truth to see.
Lift high the candle, what will be will be.
Lift high the candle, to know things as they are.
Lift high the candle, to be answered by a star.

The world may face devastation, plagues and sorrows, too.

Yet this is our salvation, the bright and shining truth:
The light cannot be extinguished, in burns within each soul.
To this it brings us: what was destroyed can be made whole.

Lift high the candle, let your voices sing.
Lift high the candle, make every bell to ring.
Lift high the candle, know you are not alone.
Lift high the candle, go forth and rebuild home.

Little Knives

L ittle knives and mighty blows,
　　　What comes of this? No one knows.
Tiny swords in mighty hands,
Strutting as though they're big and grand.

Mighty swords in lesser hands,
Wonder at the strutting band.
So strong they seem, yet is it so?
A simple question and over they go.

The rage that comes in tiny swords,
Lives destroyed with naught but words,
Yet some there stand against the storm,
And truth will through e'er comes the morn.

When mighty hands come to fail,
And show they're petty, old, and frail,
Then simple hands rise swords anew,
And voices rise and join them, too.

Betrayal

It came for those with eyes to see
    In defiance of reality.
It came for those with eyes shut tight
And left them stunned in dead of night.

Bitter shouts raised to the sky,
Riling at those who dared ask why.
Shocked and numb and lost at sea
The seekers could not let it be.

But none could change that painful blow
No matter what the truth would show.
Some retreat to despair's dark home
And more the loss as if alone.

Others stood though they could not move,
Others walked the truth to prove.
Chaos flowed from enemy hand,
Flesh and spirit against the land.

Yet truth and hope they cannot crush

No matter how it comes first blush.
Betrayal comes with crippling pain,
But evil yet will evil maim.

Numb

N othing comes to empty dawn
     And honor's held in bitter pawn.
Souls freeze to death in empty chill
And naught remains of mind or will.

A moment frozen as the heart
That has lost its sacred art
And cannot look beyond the edge
Of broken souls and deadly ledge.

Insults flow but cannot find
Purchase left in empty mind.
An empty soul bereft and numb
Sinking slowly to loss succumbs.

Yet slowly does the heart still beat
And bitter fights that brought retreat
Do not mean the war is lost
Though bitter still is the cost.

Slowly souls climb to their feet

And one by one each other meet
And so they go from day to day
And together find a new way.

Unhealed

A thousand cuts, a thousand lives,
A thousand fell to silent knives.
A cry of rage in anguish torn,
From those now left alone to mourn.

Hands have hid the knives away,
And hide the truth from light of day.
Yet, light still shines on all that's true,
And hearts have turned to see it new.

The rage it boils beneath the skin,
And noble hearts fight within.
They fight their rage because they know
Destruction's edge if they let go.

They know the cost, they know the price,
They know the bitter sacrifice.
Yet silent still, they come and come,
And the line yet forms one by one.

Yet still there is another line,

That shines within the light divine.
Another line of evil foes,
That earthly vengeance doesn't know.

Hands reach to the grieving heart,
To share the pain, yes every part.
Hands of flesh and hands of light,
That bear the tears into the night.

Spirit now and flesh combined,
And still the truth will hold the line.
While wits are sharp and battled honed,
Remember still you are not alone.

Standing Still

Do I betray by standing still?
    Upon this line? Upon this hill?
If the choice be still or to step back
Here I stand against attack.

I stand and look upon the foe.
I will not yield to any blow.
If a blow should bring me to a knee
Yet will I still refuse to flee.

Will that forward step be mine?
Or is it for me to hold the line?
First I must stand then may I go
Against the storm and any foe.

There is no back only ahead
No matter the danger or the dread.
Yet some must be that hold the line.
There we begin your task and mine.

We cannot win if we stand alone

yet we begin, standing on our own.
I do not know what that first step will be
yet here I stand I will not flee.

Price of Despair

I t is over, it is done!

    When the battle's not begun.
The soldiers fade away in the darkness of day.

Yet high upon a hill,
One stands there still.
As the darkness devours those within its powers.

That figure on its rock
Quietly took stock,
And says, "I still want my shot".

So, he bunkered down
With a smile not a frown,
And waited to see what he got.

As his wait drew long,
Another came along,
And took another rock for a seat.

And then a third came, too.

A fourth one they drew.
And kindled up a fire for the heat.

And so they passed the days
And talked about the ways
They though that this would go.

And as time passed along,
They turned into a throng
Until along came their foe.

In brashness came the foe
Because he did know,
That in despair his enemy had fled.

And the ones that came to fight
Had died in the night.
And so all his enemy was dead!

But upon that hill
Those men were waiting still
And claimed their chance of victory.

What outcome did they find?
Those men of patient mind?
Alas we must still wait for it to be

But those who surrendered to despair
Could never return there,
And so the end they'll never see.

Days of Wonder

Lightning and thunder
    And all the days of wonder
Seem to have passed us by

In the calm of the storm
Can aught be reborn
When all hope seems to fly?

But life turns strange
And swiftly fate can change
And yield to the light on high.

In dark of spirit
None will hear it
And no hope can enter in.

Yet it comes to pass
At long last,
A spark kindles within.

And hope anew

Comes to you
And a new day will begin.

An Oath

I made an oath so long ago.

My word I bound to make it so.
I honored time, and until labor freed.
But the oath will never be releasing me.

The world is bleak, the days are dark.
Yet this I watch. And this I mark.
For the wolves who howl at the door,
May invoke my oath once more.

And more the wolves who prowl within
And claim they are without one sin.
And seek to twist my oath with lies,
Will find therein their own demise.

I did not this oath lightly give,
It is one by which I live.
And so I say to the wicked
Do not think my oath spares you.

Surrender Not

K indle the fire burned to embers,
    Quench the blaze upon the heights.
Sing the song that still remembers
The truth of freedom's light.

The stillness comes from somewhere,
Though we know not when.
The rage that comes from out there.
We tame it from within.

The fire brings a brilliance,
That we can ever know.
The hearts that find resilience,
They the truth will show.

We cannot cede the battle
If we would win the war,
Though the sabers that they rattle,
Seem to come from near and far.

Despair will make us falter,

Its steps are heavy chains.
Do not take its halter,
Do not bear its reins.

It is not the anger
Against which we must stand,
But cold despair the danger,
That blames our own hand.

Turn not upon a brother,
Keep your eye fixed on the foe.
This way you will discover
Who would with you go.

Reach Into the Flood

What do you do when the words don't come?
When you can only stand, cold and numb?
What do you do when the world comes down?
And the sane around you start to drown?

You reach in the waters and find a hand,
And pull them onto the dry land.
You bring them up to your side,
And don't worry just yet about the tide.

Reach into the flood and stand your ground,
Find whoever wants to be found.
The ones that won't come, you never could save,
No matter how daring, no matter how brave.

Reach into the flood and offer a hand,
Each one that joins, the work will expand.
Reach into the flood whatever must come.
Hold on for life, you will still save some.

Drive into the waters and never look back.

Strive into the night, no matter how black.
Reach into the flood, even if it's just one,
One more beside you to greet the sun.

Spirit and Steel

It's a battle of spirit, a battle of soul.

   We fight in the body because we are still whole.
We fight in the spirit a more nebulous foe
Who has long worked his mission of anger and woe

Our weapons, the pen, the book, and the sword,
Our battlefield hope, and the soul of the world.
While blood shed may come it is a symptom of strife.
What we fight for is soul, the pulse of our life.

This soul cannot be stolen, though it can be killed,
Not by a foe, but by what our own hands will wield.
Our power is one they never can grasp.
It has no hilt, no buttstock, no haft.

Our power is truth, a bright fire within.
Our power is hope, in the future we win.
As we walk to that future, broken hearts held high,
We pass through death's valley, but our banner still flies.

Silent Accord

N
o words were spoken
  To bring them all.
No words were spoken,
Wasn't that kind of call.

One by one they came forward
And got out their guns.
Not one word was spoken
So the Beast didn't run.

The laughing Goliath of paper and straw
Crumbled to pieces at the sight of them all.
Not one word was spoken.
They knew it was war.

So down came the rifle from the mantelpiece.
Out came the ammo. Boots on the feet.
Not one word was spoken
When they killed the beast.

Not one word was spoken

Until they walked away.
Until each was returning
To rebuild the new day.

A Single Candle

T he darkness closes
    In empty days
A single candle
Is still ablaze.

The darkness howls
And swells its might
And shatters against
That tiny light.

Those lost deep in
That deadly dark
See the clash,
Hope in the spark.

The dark assails
Again and yet again
And from that light
Another begins.

The dark smothers

All it sees
But a single light
Brings it to its knees.

Yet

G leaming eyes haunt the dark,
Chill the air, in warning stark.
Yet bright the stars and kind the moon
Fall has come, yet winter soon.

Terrors haunt the restless dreams,
Fury lurks behind the beams.
Yet warm the fires and bright the glow,
Hearth and home and friends we know.

Bleak the days that seem to come.
Relentless beats the angry drum.
Yet the future is not made of these,
The future comes in falling leaves.

The future comes through winter's gloom,
And winter's start is winter's doom.
As comes the winter, so comes the spring,
Life anew it, too will bring.

So let the land have its rest.

The winter's chill both ill and blessed.
Sleeps the ground and readies the day
When Spring blows each winter away.

The Guide

A handful of hope.
A cup full of grace.
A heart with a smile.
A warrior's face.

A sword that is strong.
A shield that is true.
A heart that is bold,
Arms open to you.

An ear that will hear.
Eyes that will see.
A mind that will listen,
Even to me.

The ache of the ages,
With prices so dear,
All just to say,
"Look up, I am here."

Wrought

W rought of iron,
    Wrought of steel,
Wrought of hand,
Wrought of will.

The future is built of such as these.
The future will come as it will please.
The future is not a graven state
That comes upon those who wait.

Wrought of iron,
Wrought of steel,
Wrought of hand,
Wrought of will.

The story spun so long ago
Will keep the heart steady so,
The hand that carves the stone and wheel
Can return each day to the mill.

Wrought of iron,

Wrought of steel,
Wrought of hand,
Wrought of will.

To tear down the walls is easy to do
To tear down a place? Not so true.
A hearth, a home, and a stubborn will?
They'll find these not so easy to kill.

Wrought of iron,
Wrought of steel,
Wrought of hand,
Wrought of our will.

Against the Dark

A shadow has come over the sun
The day that is ended had only begun.
The fire that burns in a valiant ring
Burns in a soul that won't cease to sing.

Death may come marching, as he's wont to do
Death may come still, for me or for you.
Death is no friend, nor is he the foe,
The truth goes before him, inexorable. Slow.

The future we craft, they only destroy.
The work of our minds and our hand they employ.
They cannot make, nor even yet see,
That death comes for them, without you or me.

The Truth is their angel of grim empty fate,
They sally against her, far, far to late.
What comes in the future no one may see.
Yet, truth comes also to you and to me.

The truth holds a beacon, aloft and on high.

Perhaps it is that freedom may die.
Perhaps it is that freedom may live.
Yet only in light the future may give.

So lift high the light that Truth will yet bring.
Sing loud the song your heart gives to sing.
The future still comes, whatever it be.
Build in the glow, whatever we see.

Watchman

T he watchman stands against the night.
    His fire dim but still upright.
And those who come, and those who call,
Still hear his answer from the wall.

In the stillness before the storm,
When restless souls begin to mourn
And bitter souls begin to rail,
The watchman stands and does not fail.

The watchman stands, eyes ahead,
And gives an answer to all that's said.
And answers echo from soul to soul
Though the waiting takes its toll.

The watchman stands, sometimes alone,
Yet in flash of lightnings it is shone,
That other souls will with him stand,
Upon the wall that guards the land.

They Come Through Me

I stand on a hill overlooking the sea
      The invaders are coming.
They come through me.

Some say I should run; they say I should flee.
Yet invaders are coming.
They come through me.

To this land have I fled and here I will stay.
And none shall ever drive me away.

I come of my choosing.
I go of my will.
The invaders are coming.
I stand here, still.

Sometimes it is running.
Sometimes it's a fight.
Sometimes it is pain
In the dead of night.

The land they can take.
Life and wealth too.
There is far more than these they never will shake.

This land is a will they never can know.
This land is a hope they never will show.

I stand on the ridge with my face to the sea.
Invaders are coming. They come through me.

The Spark

A single spark of light
   Held gently in the hands
Against the dark of night
And terror in the lands.

A single spark of light
Gleaming in the dark
Waging battle bright
With a single spark.

A single spark of light
Shining to the eye
Sending out its might
To the empty sky.

A single spark of light
Held in every heart
Spreads throughout the night
And never will depart

Hold the Walls

Here I stand, I can do no other.

Strange the stillness in the bother.
I look to the sky and the stars still shine.
Something there is that will always be mine.

The future's a fog, but it's always been so.
Illusions have shattered, at least we know.
Yet still there are things no one ever can take.
Still there are things that never fail, only shake.

The world shifts around me, and yet I am still.
Others surround me and perhaps some always will.
We comfort the weary and so steady our souls.
There will be some to make the shattered whole.

Battle lines are now drawn against the black sky,
Lines that are written in powers on high.
The armies assembled, no flesh and his blood,
But of Princes of Spirit, against that great flood.

For us it is given to hold the high walls.

It is not for us to make the foe fall.
We stand our ground in a battle of wills.
When the battle line charges, we will hold still.

Clamor

C lamor around me, a din and a hum
      Of what's to be surrendered, what's to be done.
Shrill accusations, and "I told you so!"
When the voices were crowing their deaths to go.

Triumphant in anger, some smile up on high,
Thinking it better to lay down an die.
Frustration boils, and sears friend and foe,
And anger run rampant, an unrestrained blow.

No words come to me from the clamoring din.
The words that come to me come from within.
No sword to my hand, as yet have I found.
My words are my weapons upon this ground.

So I close out the din, and still lift my pen
A verse here and there, though I rarely know when.
When words are the right ones, the ones that ring true.
So I set them all down, it's all I can do.

And each to their own works, turns day by day,

And lets the din of anger yet slip away.
One to the building, another will fight.
Who knows when things will come right?

But the works we can manage, those we should do,
Despair is a death blow, of everything true.
What future yet comes? I cannot foresee.
There's work to be done to bring it to be.

Beacons

A ridge sloping down
    To a restless sea.
A beacon fire laid
For all to see.

Atop the ridge line
A woman in white
Her torch yet lowered
Eyes searching the night.

The ships come from nothing,
Forged in the gloom,
Silently parting
The wild ocean spume.

No ghosts do these carry,
Nor men made of flesh,
But hollow breasted horrors
Steer them to rest.

An army of Soldiers

With their souls held in pawn,
Driven by masters
Whose existence they scorn.

She raises the torch,
For a breath, to the sky
In open defiance of those
Coming to die.

The torch touches tinder,
The beacon alight
Its warning blazes
Defiance so bright.

And all along
The ridgeline so still,
Spring answering blazes
In each ridge and rill.

From each copse of trees
From every small cove,
From every high hill
And every cool grove.

No word has been spoken
When boat touches shore.
No word is yet needed
As beacon fires roar.

Future in a Candle

What is the future? Is it something we can see?
We cannot see the future, only watch it come to be.
So lift high your candle, Let it flicker in the night.
It will not be extinguished, not this tiny light.

Others come together, a candle in each hand
And a wave of fire sweeps across the land.
A fire that burns nothing, but sheds light for all to see.
A hundred thousand candles, lift high in silent memory.

Will victory come with them? Or will the fight be slow?
That future we can discover, but now we cannot know.
We only can march forward, with a candle in our hand,
Each step a battle, for home and hearth and land.

They cannot snuff each candle. They cannot find them all.
The light that shines the brightest, is the sum of them all.
A single candle gutters, but another takes its place.
A silent greeting mutters, from another stubborn face.

And amid the sea of candles, another throng is found,

A throng that walks in spirit, and in spirit it is bound.
There the battle rages, as candles spread apace.
Light has been kindled, as we this battle face.

To us it has been given, to see the future through,
To us it has been given, to build and build anew.
Whether we can see the victory of the battle's final blow,
Or think the world has ended, there is yet more to show.

So lift high your candle. Let it flicker in the night.
They cannot all be shuttered, Not so many lights.
Never fear the darkness. It will end in day.
The future is before us. Let us bind the way.

One More Dawn

C up your hands before you,
    Catch a tiny spark of joy,
A little piece of hope
That's all the saints employ.

A tiny piece of hope,
Friends drawing near.
Perhaps we're far away,
Yet we are still here.

When all you feel is empty,
And the rain's enough to drown.
Turn your collar up and then
Lift eyes that once were down.

Alone you do not wander,
A spark yet shows the way.
And we here stand beside you.
Though we are far away.

Though you yet are weary,

Though the burdens still be strong.
Light yet stands before you,
And night gives way to dawn.

Knees

S ometimes you fight upon your knees.

    Sometimes you're rocked on stormy seas.
Sometimes you cannot come to stand
Either on the sea or on the land.

Yet on your knees is not the end,
Through bitter foe and angry friend.
When ground grows still beneath your feet
And with full courage the future meet.

You find that friends and foes come to,
Some to fail, some still ring true.
And some you bring back from their edge,
Pull them back from oblivion's ledge.

Then from your knees you come to stand
And others, too, come hand in hand.
A wall of souls against the dark,
A thousand fires brightly stark.

The Storm is not Forever

The storm clouds are coming,
They blot the sun from the sky
The thunder tears the heavens
The lightning blinds the eye.

But the storm is not forever.
No storm could ever be.
Though it wreak devastation
And shatter all we see.

The storm is not forever
And we will carry through
The storm will below itself out
And we will build anew.

The storm is not forever,
What remains we've yet to see.
But the storm is not forever.
A new day there will be.

Rhythems of Life

C up the spark in your hand
    Release it to the night.
When the darkness demands,
Turn it to the light.

Wend a path made of stone,
Through a forest made of fog
Carry all that you own,
And dance the river bog.

Alone it all begins,
But never stays that way.
Together life must end
And hope comes home to stay.

Take the tool in your hand,
No work save comes from you
Turn your face to the land,
There is much still left to do.

No rest yet comes with dawning,

No prizes come by day,
Yet home and house aborning
Will not quickly fade away.

Hope leads with gentle brilliance,
Through shadows of the tombs,
Yet in the heart's resilience,
The future comes in bloom.

Those Who Build

L
ift high the torch of freedom
  To echo heaven's light
Against the smoking darkness
And the creeping blight.

The smoke, bound tight with curses,
Clings and fosters fears.
Yet still the spark of heaven
Lights uplifted tears.

Through fear and fire we wander
Against the far-flung foe,
Yet each new voice has lifted
A song of truth to flow.

Each song wends through the darkness
Driving back the gloom.
Yet slow comes the victory
And fast seems the doom.

Yet doom has stood before us

Time and time again,
And hope yet lingers o'er us
And aid beyond our ken.

We will not fall to devils
We will not fall to flood
We will not fall to monsters
Who harm us 'for our good'.

What enemies can sunder
We can build anew.
We build over, around, and under,
And weave truth and freedom through.

Hands

S oil rich within my hands
    Heat unyielding in shimmering bands.
Plant the seeds and help them grow
To feed us all as ages flow.

Stone and trowel, steady will
Row on row rises still.
Home or hearth or guardian wall
My hands still lay them one and all.

Pick and stone, hammer and steel,
Mine the rock and bring it to heel.
Bring the dark into the light,
My hands bring the ore of futures bright.

Blend the ore, black the gold
Unbind the pieces, their treasures unfold
Forge the bits to something new
And craft the future from me to you.

Look Up

L ook to the sky
    Look to the stars
They can't take us over
They can't take what's ours.

The work of our hands,
We can always redo.
The things in our minds
We pass down to you.

The will to the striving
They never will break.
The hope in our labors
They never can take.

The fire that burns
In every free soul
Is something they never
Can see nor control.

They think in our spirits

We are like them,
Yet we know the truth:
We are still men.

No machine to dance
To a street grinder's tune.
No dog to lie lazy,
Then howl at the moon.

We look to the sky
And reach to the stars,
And they can't understand
What makes the sky ours.

Prometheus

R eturn the fire to the sky.
　　　The Gift shines bright.
The hand of God
Stands against the night.

Return the fire to the sky.
Hear the roaring of the night.
Demon rage the light abhors,
The monsters below out their fright.

Return the fire to the sky
Prometheus bled not in vain
Greater hands than his tormentors
Have lifted up the flame.

New Beginnings

The spark of life that starts all things
Unwinds and flies on blazing wings,
Eyes turned up into the night
See its radiance take to flight.

In days of old this hope still grew,
And each bright dawn it sparks anew.
A promise of bright hope to come,
To all the edges of Christendom.

Though dark the night that bars the way,
It must yet yield to dawning day.
And bright the flight that begins anew
And sparkles on the glistening dew.

Future

D ance with me to the future,
    Sing with me to the past.
Weave them deftly together
So eternity shall last.

The present is but a flicker
The Past a looming storm,
But in that moment of brightness,
Eternity is born.

A word, a smile, a gesture,
What its reach we can't know.
When any heart be uplifted,
And any the future show.

So sing the joy of the moment,
And sing till the sorrow is past.
The future in shadows is written,
Yet the future, in brilliance be cast.

Bright

B right the days
      Bright the sun
Bright and warm
The work be done.

Bright the night.
Bright the moon.
In sleepy light
And slumber soon.

Bright the fire.
Bright the Home
Hear the lyre
No longer roam.

Bright the heart,
Bright the soul.
Bright the voices
That weave them whole

A Blessing

A table laid with food and drink.
    A chair to sit and rest and think.
A fire lit so you can see.
A simple gift of hospitality.

If I could give these simple things
I'd have them here what e'er life brings.
Your heart is torn, and things are bleak,
And there seems nothing left to seek.

I leave a song, to ease your heart,
A small thing, somewhere to start.
A prayer of hope for something true.
May blessings yet, shower you.

May you find a brighter day.
May you find hope along the way.
May your days be true and long.
May you find a joyful song.

Lift your head, look to the sun.

There is a day just begun.

What will it bring, we shall see.

May there be hope that comes to be.

About Author

I am old enough to worry about growing old gracefully, but not old enough to be graceful about it yet. After a stint in the Army and a longer stint as a geophysicist, with some bouts of IT work and other odds and ends thrown in the work, I've finally settled down on 10 acres with my family.

All along the way there have been stories, some big and some small. Some that are forever lost on 5.25 inch floppies (the ones that actually flopped!) and are probably the better for it. Now, these stories are starting to come out of trunks, and the depth of my mind and get themselves finished and find their way into the world, along with a fair few new ones. After all, stories never come alone. They always bring worlds with them, and sometimes those worlds bring friends of their own. And poetry and songs. Those that I had always thought would be just for me, but life is sometimes strange in delightful ways.

I hope you have enjoyed this book and that it has brought you a glimmer of the joy poetry has brought me throughout my own life. Feel free to reach out to me either on my websites or by e-mail, I can't guarantee I'll respond to everything but I will try.

Publisher: www.wyrdbardtales.com
Personal: www.dreaminginplot.com
heather@dreaminginplot.com

Also By

Spiral of Worlds Multiverse
Whirlwind of Stars by Heather Strickler

Comming Soon:
Persistant Powers Universe
Bearskin